Food, Drink and History

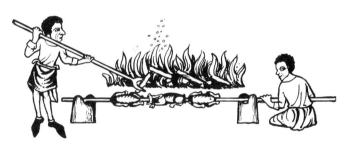

*Medieval spit. From the Luttrell Psalter,
a 14th century manuscript*

FOOD,
DRINK

Line drawings by Pamela Adams

DAVID & CHARLES · NEWTON ABBOT

STEPHEN USHERWOOD

AND

HISTORY

ISBN 0 7153 5657 7

Set in Bembo and printed in Great Britain by
Redwood Press Limited Trowbridge and London
for David & Charles (Publishers) Limited
South Devon House Newton Abbot Devon

Contents

An Eskimo wife sews a skin covering on to a kayak

Opposite: Eskimo handicrafts are now world-famous. This fine carving of two Eskimos hauling up a seal is by Simonee of Povungnetuk

1
Breakfast

Every morning we 'break our fast', not having eaten since the previous evening. Breakfast for us is often a hurried meal because we know there will be plenty to eat later in the day. There is seldom any need for us to go without food, but in early times long fasts between meals were often a necessity. This is still true in some very hot and very cold regions. Until recently the Eskimos of Greenland were accustomed to fast for fourteen days at a time. Though they lived on the world's largest island, little was known about their way of life or of the geography of their country until the 1930s. Then British explorers arrived accompanied by men of the Royal Air Force with some small reconnaissance aircraft. One of the pilots wanted to learn how to use an Eskimo kayak. There was none big enough for him—Eskimo men are not tall—so he asked them to build one to fit him, but was told that they were not hungry; the skins needed for the hull of his new kayak could only be taken from seals killed for food, and there would be no hunting for a fortnight.

Later, when breakfast was over and all had recovered—the meal had taken two days—work began. First a wooden framework was fashioned with knives out of drift wood. Then two layers of sealskin, each separately stitched together with seal sinew, were fitted over the frame. Unneeded trimmings of skin were gobbled up while the men worked. Nothing was wasted. To these Greenlanders, who lived by hunting and fishing, wild life was precious; no creature was needlessly killed, even though there might be a long wait before they could break their fast once more.

From prehistoric times those people who lived by hunting have always employed dogs, and dog bones have been found lying among the remains of all the earliest inhabited sites from Greenland to Australia. Perhaps it is because dogs have been the friends of man for so many hundreds of thousands of years that they still are the most popular of all domestic pets. Probably they were the first wild animals to be tamed and given useful work to do. Today most dogs would starve if their masters did not feed them; in ancient times the masters would have starved if their hunting dogs had not scented out their prey and helped to retrieve it.

Some of the first historical accounts of food shortages afflicting whole nations are given in the Bible, where there is a description of a seven-year famine in Egypt and all the other lands at the eastern end of the Mediterranean about the year 2000 BC. The Hebrews were then living in the land now called Israel, partly as farmers and partly as herdsmen, moving

Hunting the stag with hounds in medieval days.
From Queen Mary's Psalter, a 14th century manuscript

Egyptian plough
drawn by oxen,
about 2000 BC.
It had no cutting edge, but the
wooden shaft was dragged through the soil

their flocks of cattle, sheep and goats from one pasture to another according to the season. Sometimes drought scorched their grasslands or a plague of locusts passed by, eating every green leaf and blade of grass. In such an emergency even the locusts afforded food. The Hebrews, to whom many foods were forbidden, were allowed to eat them. As the third book of the Bible says:

> *You may eat every kind of great locust, every kind of long-headed locust, every kind of green locust. Every other kind of teeming winged creature that has four legs you shall regard as vermin.*

> *(Leviticus 11, 22-23).*

At one time the rain-bearing east wind blighted the wheat fields of Egypt and all the surrounding countries for seven years in succession. Fortunately for the Egyptians the Pharaoh's chief minister advised them during the previous seven years of good harvest to store up all the surplus grain; so when the harvest failed they had enough not only for themselves, but for their neighbours; 'all the world' sent to Egypt for corn. Among those who came were the sons of Jacob, little knowing that the Pharaoh's wise minister was their brother Joseph whom many years before they had secretly left to die in the desert. Joseph,

Locust

having recognised them, though they did not know him, accused them of being spies sent to plan an invasion of Egypt. When they told him that their father was still alive and had another son, Benjamin, who was much younger than they were, he sent them back with enough sacks of corn on their pack animals to save Jacob and Benjamin and all their people from starvation, but with a stern command that they must bring Benjamin with them to Egypt to prove that they were not spies but really the sons of Jacob. The thought of parting with Benjamin made Jacob very sorrowful; hoping that the Pharaoh's minister might change his mind, he sent him as a present some of the tasty foods for which his country was famous, a little honey, pistachio nuts and almonds.

Eventually Jacob went to Egypt and was re-united with all his sons, and Joseph gave them some of the best land in Egypt to live on. Many years later the Egyptians began to persecute the Hebrews, and to escape from oppression Moses led his people out into the desert. There they lived the life of nomads for forty years and then took possession of the land where Jacob had lived; to them, coming in from the desert, it was a land 'flowing with milk and honey'.

The mysterious blight that had destroyed the wheat crops in Joseph's time, now called rust, was not understood until modern times. It is a fungus that is still liable to settle on the stalks of wheat and suck all the goodness that should go up into the grain. Its red spores multiply quickly in wet weather and float up into the clouds, sometimes causing red rain and turning rivers to the colour of blood.

The ancient Greeks and Romans also suffered from the same blight on their crops as the Hebrews and Egyptians, and they noticed that it came in wet cold weather. They therefore erected many magnificent temples to the sun god Apollo, believing that if they offered him sacrifices and prayers he would no longer hide his face in the grey rain clouds but send fine weather and bring healthy crops.

To acquire new wheat-growing lands became one of the chief objects of the Romans. There was not enough wheat grown in Italy to feed the city of Rome with its hundreds of thousands of inhabitants, and they brought wheat by the shipload from Sardinia and from North Africa. When the greatest of the Roman generals, Julius Caesar, was conquering Gaul (the land now called France) he found that the Celtic tribes who were proving such obstinate foes were receiving grain from Britain. Wheat was in fact Britain's first major export, and Caesar saw among other things the advantages to be gained by making the wheat lands in the south and east of the island part of the Roman empire. His two attempts at invasion failed, and the native kings continued to grow rich by selling grain to Europe. Between AD 10 and 40 the royal mint at Colchester

Hadrian's Wall as it probably was in
Roman times, from a picture by Alan Sorrell

*Gold stater of Cunobelin showing
ear of wheat, about AD 10–40*

issued gold coins called staters
that had a picture of an ear of
wheat on one side and on the
other the first four letters of the
king's name, Cunobelinus.
Later, when the Romans had
conquered the country up to the Scottish border, they sent to
their garrisons along Hadrian's Wall grain grown in what is
now Lincolnshire.

A grain of wheat contains within it the greatest quantity of
food in the smallest space—all the carbohydrates, fats, proteins,
vitamins and minerals that the human body needs. Brown
bread, made with flour from which no part of the grain has been
extracted, is the most nutritious food and to live on brown
bread and water would be a hardship only because it would be
so boring not to taste anything different. It was therefore most
important to learn the cause of rust. It took many years of
patient study and observation to find out why the disease kept
returning even when the wheat was dead, and at last it was
discovered that the rust was harboured by an evergreen bush
called barberry, or berberis, and that enough rust spores could
breed on one bush to destroy wheat over an area of ten square
miles. The first rust-resistant seed grain was bred in Australia,
and now all over the world scientists are busy breeding new
kinds of wheat.

Another great improvement in wheat also started in Australia.
In 1860 a farmer in Victoria noticed an odd-looking plant of
wheat in one of his fields. It had a heavy ear with a square top
and a strong short stalk and when he bred from it all its grains
produced the same type of plant. It 'bred true', as biologists say.
Most wheat had long stalks that were often damaged by wind

and rain. If all went well until after harvest time the long stalks were useful for thatching roofs, but many farmers wanted wheat that had short stalks and heavy ears. This stood up to bad weather and could be reaped by combine-harvesters.

The men who first learned how to grow grain were probably herdsmen of Asia who, like the Australian farmer, found wild grasses with unusually big seeds in their mountain pastures and by planting these in separate plots at last bred the plants we call wheat, oats, barley and rye. All of them made tasty bread or biscuits. It was from the men of the hills that the peoples of the plains obtained the seed which cropped so well in the deep well-watered soil beside the rivers Ganges, Tigris, Euphrates and Nile. In America maize, which is sometimes called Indian corn, probably became a food plant in the same way; it was once a tall kind of wild grass. From it the flakes now served at breakfast time are manufactured. The grain forms a heavy cob sheathed in a close-fitting husk. Under this covering it cannot ripen without plenty of hot sun. Ripe maize is a golden brown colour and as hard as flint, but if the cobs are harvested early, when the grain is pale gold, they can be boiled until they are soft and sweet to eat.

Maize was cultivated in America many thousands of years before Christopher Columbus began his explorations. The earliest signs of it, dating from 4500 BC, were found in the Bat Cave in New Mexico. By AD 1519, when the Spaniards under Cortes invaded Mexico, they found that maize was one of the foods that the Aztecs there relied upon most. In South

The Aztec god of rain carrying a maize plant. From a hand-painted manuscript found in Mexico

America too the Spanish conquerors found that where the climate was hot and dry maize was a favourite crop. It does not make bread, but, ground to a fine powder, mixed with water and then cooked like a pancake, it is good to eat warm; cold, it quickly becomes inedible.

The Spaniards who sailed to Mexico and Peru were adventurers, eager to make fortunes in new lands. There was little of value in the New World that they did not attempt to take home. They were both inquisitive and acquisitive. First, they wanted to know where the gold and silver mines were, and to take possession of them, but they also saw that maize was a plant likely to prosper in the climate and soil of Spain, where the summers are very hot. The few bags of golden seed that they shipped to Andalusia proved more valuable than all the precious metal that they mined. From Spain maize was carried to other Mediterranean countries, to Africa, and to China. In South Africa corn cobs were called *milje* by the Dutch colonists, and *mealies* by the English.

In North America Indian corn saved the lives of the settlers who in 1620 crossed the Atlantic in *Mayflower* and landed near Cape Cod. On arrival they found the Indian villages deserted because the inhabitants had been killed by a mysterious disease.

In the Indian's huts were baskets of grain. It was too late in the year to sow any corn, and that first winter they had to live on the stores they had brought. Many, weakened by hunger, died, possibly of the same disease that had afflicted the Indians. Fortunately in the spring they were visited by two Indians, Samoset and Squanto, who, to their astonishment, could speak some English. They had

A stalk of maize

learnt it from sailors who had called on that coast for water and had taken them to London and back. The Indians showed the *Mayflower* men how to plant the maize in little hillocks. Squanto also taught them to set fish traps on the shore and to use the fish as fertiliser for the maize. This meant that men had to guard the corn plots day and night to scare away all the wild animals that tried to get at the fish. In the autumn they gathered in a good crop and decided to celebrate the occasion with a religious service of thanksgiving and a feast. Early in November the men went out shooting and brought home wild geese, turkeys and duck. The Indians gave them venison and they made wine from wild grapes. Roast goose reminded them of the friends and relatives whom they had left in exile in Holland, for there St Martin's Day, 11 November, was kept as a feast day and roast goose was the principal dish. Long afterwards Abraham Lincoln, as President of the United States, decreed that the fourth Thursday in November should be observed as National Thanksgiving Day, and now Americans all over the world keep this as a holiday in memory of the *Mayflower* Pilgrims.

Plymouth still commemorates the departure of the Pilgrim Fathers from the Barbican, the old quarter of the city, to board the 'Mayflower' on their famous voyage to a new life and a new world in America

2
Dinner

Hams being smoked
in a chimney

What have you for dinner today? That is a question that has been asked of every wife and mother since ancient times. Today there are many countries where almost every family expects the answer to include meat, poultry or fish, vegetables and a sweet, but it has not always been so. In Britain in Queen Elizabeth I's reign there was a saying:

From Christmas to May
Weak cattle decay.

Nobody knew how to keep more than a few of their cattle, sheep and chicken alive during the first three months of the year, and that meant no fresh meat for dinner. The carcases of animals slaughtered before Christmas were stored in brine, or, in the case of hams, smoked in the chimney, and kept for use until spring. Salt meat was not very palatable, and all sorts of spices and flavourings were used to improve the taste. There was a great demand for pepper, nutmegs, cloves, and cinnamon.

All through the Middle Ages fresh meat in winter was food for kings, and their favourite meat was venison. William the Conqueror provided himself with a vast new hunting reserve, still known as the New Forest. This is more heathland than forest, not far to the south-west of Winchester, the capital of the Norman kings, and on their visits to England they could be sure of getting a good day's hunting there. Red deer, the largest wild creatures still left in Britain, then bred in the south, and on days when they could not be found, there were plenty of fallow deer, smaller creatures but fleet of foot. The royal hounds, specially bred for speed and strength, brought the stags to bay so that the king and his courtiers could shoot them with bows and arrows. Forest-dwellers who bred dogs were regarded by the nobility with great suspicion. A clever dog could be a great help to a deer poacher, and any poor man's dog seen chasing deer would be immediately mutilated and his owner punished. Smaller game like hares and rabbits, however, could be taken by the poor, to whom they were very welcome.

Wild fowl were another source of fresh meat. On marsh land and river estuaries there were duck, mallard, teal and widgeon, as well as migrating geese and swans. To hunt among the vast flights of such birds, then a common sight, the nobility had falcons specially trained, but poor men used their skill with dogs, nets and decoys.

A knight with two companions and two dogs carries a falcon on his gloved hand. From a 16th century book of falconry

Tame geese were kept on most village greens and provided many a good dinner. They eat a great deal of grass and had to be watched by children to keep them away from growing crops, but they were useful watchdogs, giving the first warning, night and day, of the approach of strangers. Goose down provided the warmest of beds, and their wing feathers the quills needed by bowmen for their arrows and by clerks for pens. Some owners became very fond of their geese and treated them as pets, as this nonsensical old nursery rhyme shows. A goose girls sings:

Quill pen

> *Goosey, Goosey Gander, whither shall I wander?*
> *Upstairs, downstairs and in my Lady's chamber,*
> *There I met an old man who would not say his prayers,*
> *I took him by the left leg and threw him downstairs.*

Old dining customs are still kept up by Oxford and Cambridge colleges and by societies of lawyers called Lincoln's Inn, Gray's Inn and the Middle and Inner Temple.

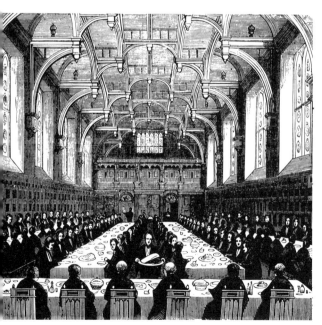

19th century term dinner in the Middle Temple Hall

In the dining hall at the Middle Temple the old procedure is followed on every guest night. When the Benchers and more important guests arrive, the rest of the company stand and wait while they go in procession to high table. There, before anyone sits down, grace is said and when those at high table have finished their meal, all stand again and another grace is said before the guests leave. In the Middle Ages, when every man's rank in society was carefully observed, each guest 'knew his place' in such processions. An earl would take precedence over a baron, and so on.

'High table' is so called because it was placed on a dais at the far end of the hall from the entrance, so that the chief guests sat facing down the hall towards the doors and got the best view of what went on below, where the tables were parallel to the side walls, leaving passage ways for the servants bringing in the various dishes.

The tables in medieval times were not solid pieces of furniture as they are now, but heavy planks laid across trestles. We still speak of tables 'groaning with food'. Of course our tables do sometimes creak, but they never groan as these movable tables did. High table guests now have chairs, but in the old days they had only benches without backs, as those sitting in the body of the hall still do. Benches, planks and trestles could easily be stacked against the side walls when the feast was over, then dancing, play-acting, and acrobatic displays could be enjoyed.

To have a big hall where all a nobleman's retainers, or all the teachers and students in a college, could eat together and enjoy

Medieval acrobat, accompanied by tabor (on left) and pipe. From a 14th century manuscript, 'The Decretals of Gregory IX'

themselves was an ambition which medieval architects knew how to satisfy. Roof beams long enough to stretch from one side wall to the other were obviously too expensive and too difficult to get. Shorter timbers would have needed pillars to support them and these would have got in the way of guests, so, like bridge builders, they constructed the most wonderful arches in timber to span the floor space and hold up the high-pitched roof. The magnificent timber ceiling of the Middle Temple hall is a replica of one destroyed by bombing in the Second World War. Westminster Hall, once the banqueting hall of the kings of England, was given a lofty new timber roof by Richard II that set the fashion for many others.

Medieval and Tudor dining halls were usually separate buildings with a floor at or near ground level. Their doors had to stand open for the servants to bring in dishes from the kitchen, and guests suffered great discomfort from cold

The Great Hall of Hampton Court Palace

Boar's Head

draughts. They usually had to wear the same clothes indoors as they did out.

One way of reducing the cold was to cover the bare walls with tapestries embroidered with scenes from the Bible or from Greek and Roman myths. This was done in the Tudor hall at Hampton Court. Other walls were covered with beautiful linen-fold panelling.

Another improvement was to have a wooden screen built across the end of the hall, pierced by passage-ways, and then above the screen to build a gallery for musicians and entertainers. From here fanfares were blown to announce important guests or the arrival of some special delicacy from the kitchen like a boar's head. This was a favourite dish at Christmas time, and is still served at Queen's College, Oxford, to the accompaniment of music and the singing of a special carol.

Laying the table was a simple business. Sometimes a cloth was spread. Instead of a plate a thick slice of bread called a trencher was set before each person. Dishes of meat mixed with vegetables and gravy were then brought in, each with enough for eight to twelve people. When they were set in the middle of the table the diners reached out with their fingers to take their share.

If there was a joint to carve, the carver held out each portion on the end of his knife and the guest took it off with his fingers. To be carver was an honourable task and a skilled one. The poet Geoffrey Chaucer, who lived in the reign of Richard II, says in praise of a squire that he carved at table in the presence of his father, meaning that his father was proud of the way his son performed.

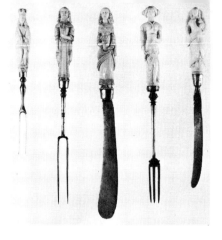

The diners, having put their portions on their trenchers, held them down with their fingers while they cut pieces off with their own knives. To get gravy from the dish they would dip in some bread. Chaucer describes a Prioress who could do this so skilfully that not a drop of gravy fell on the tablecloth or elsewhere. None the less eating without forks was a messy business and to wash their hands people would either go to a sideboard set with basins, ewers of water and towels, or ask pages to bring the basins to table. Forks were first used in Italy, but did not come into use in England until Stuart times.

When the meal was over, the trenchers were naturally soaked with gravy and the juice of meat and vegetables, and it was customary to sweep them off the tables into large baskets or carry them in the table cloth to the door of the hall, where there would be a queue of poor people waiting patiently to take in their hands what was regarded as a most welcome gift. In Tudor times, when trenchers of wood or pewter came into general use, guests were expected to leave plenty of food uneaten so that the scrapings could be given to the poor. If you left no scraps, you were expected to throw a small coin into the plate to be given to the poor. We still use the phrase 'a good trencherman', meaning a man who has a good appetite and eats heartily.

Some of the kitchens, like the dining halls, were magnificent. Two of the finest still stand almost as they did when they were first built—the abbot's kitchen at Glastonbury in Somerset, and the bishop's kitchen at Durham. Both were built of stone to reduce the danger of fire, and are bigger than many modern houses, being 36 feet across. The Glastonbury kitchen has a high conical roof to take away the heat and smells of cooking, and the Durham one is eight-sided with four big fireplaces where meat could be roasted on spits turning in front of log fires.

An account of the Christmas dinner provided by Tynemouth Priory in Northumberland gives a good idea of what medieval guests might expect to eat. The priory owned the manor of Whitley and some time before Christmas the steward there was instructed to prepare food, drink and beds for servants from Tynemouth and other priory estates.

To Whitley the prior sent men from the manor of Preston and the hayward and carter from the manor of Seaton, together with the keelers who rowed the priory barge, four threshers and a winnowing man or woman. On arrival they were given food, drink and lodging for two days and nights.

A 15th century illustration showing the King of Portugal with his bishops and courtiers entertaining John of Gaunt to dinner. The royal arms of England hand on the wall behind his guest. The table bears knives and trenchers and musicians pipe in the gallery

The amount each had to eat varied according to rank. The squires had whole hens, one between two; and those of lesser rank half a hen between two, with roast meat. The cowherds were given roast meat and cheese. The steward was also instructed to give all his guests good ale and good beds, one between two.

The Christmas holiday used to be much longer than it is now—twelve days, in fact, and a special cake was baked for 'the twelfth day of Christmas', or Twelfth Night. The cook put in a single bean and a single pea and a number of cloves, and when the family of the lord of the manor, together with his guests and servants, were assembled, the cake was brought in and put on the table. The host cut it into equal slices, one for each person present; the one who found the bean in his slice became 'King of the Feast', the one who found the pea became 'Queen', and those who got the cloves were 'courtiers'. If a woman got the bean, she had to pretend to be a man and the fun became all the greater.

The 'King' then dressed up in royal robes with crown and sceptre, even though in real life he might be only a servant. He could order his 'subjects' to play his favourite game, to dance, sing songs, recite poems, play charades or anything else that might add to the fun of the feast.

Twelfth Night celebration. From an early 19th century journal

This custom of cutting 'the Twelfth cake', as it was called, flourished until quite modern times. It is mentioned by two famous writers, Samuel Pepys and William Thackeray.

Here are some instructions from a medieval book on how to behave at dinner.

> *Bite not thy bread and lay it down,*
> *That is no courtesy to use in Town,*
> *But break as much as thou wilt eat;*
> *The remnant to the poor thou shalt let.*
> *Never let thy cheek be made too great*
> *With morsel of bread that thou shalt eat;*
> *If any man speak that time to thee,*
> *How shalt thou answer? It will not be!*
> *Thou shalt not laugh or speak or sing*
> *While thy mouth be full of meat or drink,*
> *Nor sup with great sounding,*
> *Nor blow on thy dish or meat.*
> *Let not thy spoon stand in the dish,*
> *Whether thou be served with flesh or fish.*
> *Also eschew to foul the table cloth with thy knife.*
> *Never put thy meat into thy mouth with thy knife.*
> *Cleanse not thy teeth while sitting at meat,*
> *Either with your knife or with a stick.*
> *Wipe thou thy mouth well on thy napkin*
> *Before and after thou shalt drink ale or wine.*
> *If thy own dog doth thee scrape and claw,*
> *That is held unwise by men who know.*
> *Lean not on elbow at thy meat.*
> *Dip not thy thumb or fingers in thy drink.*
> *Never tell thou at table any tale*
> *To harm or shame thy fellow guest.*

3
Sugar and Spice

If we found that somebody had added sugar to the gravy for
dinner, we should not like it at all, but in the Middle Ages this
was one of the uses to which sugar was put. With various spices,
it was a flavouring for meat dishes, and in ancient times, before
sugar was known in Europe, honey, obtained from either wild
or tame bees, was used. The first Europeans to discover sugar
were the soldiers of Alexander the Great, the young King of
Macedonia, who, between 333 and 323 BC, conquered all the
lands from Greece to the borders of India. When his men
entered northern India, they were astonished to find what they
described as 'solid honey not made by bees'. From that time on
limited quantities of sugar were brought by traders from the
east to Europe. Europeans had no nearer source of supply until
the Moors invaded Sicily and Spain in the 700s and planted
sugar cane there. Eight hundred years later Christopher
Columbus took sugar cane to the West Indies on his second
voyage. The climate there was right for it, but for a long time
few settlers could face the expense and labour of extracting
sugar from the cane, which grows even more strongly than
maize and when ripe is over ten feet tall.

Above: the caravel of Columbus

26

Even in Mediterranean countries cutting and gathering such a crop was heavy work in the heat of summer. The stacks of cane had to be stripped of their leaves and crushed between millstones until the watery juice inside had all been squeezed out. The juice then had to be boiled in big vats to drive off the water in steam, a slow process, leaving sugar crystals and a residue of black treacly molasses, a name derived from the Latin word for honey, though the treacle was not nearly so nice as honey to eat. The sugar was crystallised in moulds that gave each lump the shape of a cone with a rounded top, called a sugar-loaf, since it resembled half a loaf of bread standing on end. To get pieces of sugar to put in drinks or powdery sugar for sweetening dishes the cook worked on a sugar-loaf with a tiny axe and scraper. There are two famous 'sugar-loaf' mountains in South America, so-called because of their shape and distinctive position, standing quite apart from the surrounding country. One is at the entrance to the harbour of Rio de Janeiro in Brazil and the other is Potosi in Bolivia.

The sugar mill, a 16th century engraving. The cane is cut and the syrup is extracted and poured into moulds

*Gathering the maple sap
in the Canadian province of Quebec*

It was in the Portuguese colony of Brazil that the sugar cane industry was first established and from there it spread to the Spanish, French, Dutch and British colonies in the Caribbean. To do the hard work of extraction in the tropical heat the planters employed negro slaves imported from West Africa, where traders bought them from African chieftains. The best of these slaves came from the Ashanti country, now part of Ghana. An English sugar planter named Christopher Codrington wrote to the Board of Trade in London in 1701:

They are not only the best of our slaves, but are really all born heroes. There never was a rascal or coward of that nation. My father, who had studied all kinds of negroes for forty-five years, used to say: 'No man deserves one of them who would not treat him like a friend rather than a slave'.

By no means all slave owners were like the Codringtons and, because labour was comparatively cheap, nobody thought out improved methods of manufacturing sugar. Eventually Parliament compelled the planters to set their slaves free. Today none of the West Indian islands are colonies any longer but many are still 'sugar islands' and the people, especially in Cuba, live almost entirely by growing sugar to sell abroad. Britain is one of their best customers, since more sugar is eaten here, either as a flavouring for food or in sweets, than in any other country in the world, an average of nearly half a pound a week for every man, woman and child.

Settlers in Canada and the country just to the south of it found another source of sugar—a particular kind of maple tree. Every spring they went out into the woods and drilled holes in the trunks and hammered spigots into them. Through these dripped the clear watery sap and so a bucket was hung on each to catch it. The buckets were collected and taken to sheds where the sap was put into vats and boiled till enough moisture had been driven off, leaving a clear golden syrup or a brown sugar. This is still done every year.

The word 'spring' is not a good description of the woods at sugaring time. Apart from the dark pines there is not a leaf or green shoot to be seen, and the ground is covered with thick snow, but the forest people know that the sap is rising in the trees because at night they hear the skeins of wild geese flying over, honking loudly. The birds know it is time for their annual migration from the warm south to their spring breeding grounds in the far north. The smell of the steam rising through the roofs of the refining sheds and curling over the tree tops is delicious. Parties of children gather from all the farms to enjoy the first taste of the sugar and to gaze at the sugar icicles that form as the steam condenses on every branch and twig. No wonder that the leaf of the maple tree has become the national badge of Canada!

Canadian flag

The discovery that sugar equal in quality to cane sugar could be obtained from sugar beet was not made until the 18th century. This crop was not widely grown till 1807, when the Prussians fought Napoleon, the Emperor of the French, were beaten and had to make peace. They at once found themselves blockaded by the British navy and unable to buy either sugar or coffee. They could find no substitute for coffee, but they planted sugar beet on a big scale. The extraction process then took twenty-five tons of beet to yield a ton of sugar, but now it takes only five tons, and one third of all the sugar consumed in the world comes from beet.

It was in 1917 that the British, with their supplies of cane sugar cut off by the German submarine blockade, began to cultivate the sugar beet. The crop has to be protected from frost while it is being transported from the fields to the pro-cessing factory, and the extraction must be made quickly, otherwise beet consume their own sugar and are useless. Between harvests these factories stand idle, but so great is the demand of the British for sweet foods of all kinds that this expensive process is still profitable.

Just as some people do not like sweets or sweet foods, so others do not like food flavoured with pepper, cloves, nutmeg, or mace. Yet in the past the passion for these spices has been so keen that high prices were paid for quite small quantities. The Romans were particularly fond of pepper, which they obtained by trade through Egypt, where the Arabians marketed the pepper that their ships brought across the Indian Ocean from the Malabar coast. Even in the last days of the Roman Empire there were supplies of pepper corns in Italy. In AD 409, when

| *Sugar beet* | *Pepper corns* | *Cloves* | *Nutmeg* |

Alaric the Goth threatened to sack the city of Rome, the price
he demanded for sparing it was:

   5,000 lb of gold   4,000 robes of silk
  30,000 lb of silver   3,000 pieces of fine scarlet cloth
         and 3,000 lb of pepper corns.

The Romans found the pepper corns the most difficult part of
this ransom to collect.

Pepper corns are the dried berries of a vine that can only
grow in a tropical climate. If the berries are picked unripe the
drying process makes them black, and when ground the pepper
is black and very hot. If the berries are picked ripe, and the
outer part rubbed off, the pepper is white and its taste is much
milder.

During the Middle Ages pepper from the west coast of
India, and cloves, cinnamon and other spices from the East
Indies, were brought by traders to ports at the eastern end of
the Mediterranean. On the way they were bought and sold
several times and the prices steadily rose. From Syria and
Egypt the ships and galleys of Venice carried them to Italy;

*A spice ship
of Venice*

from there, packed on the backs of horses and mules, they travelled through the Alps to Germany and northern Europe.

Shakespeare, in his play *The Merchant of Venice*, describes what it felt like to be in this sea-borne trade. The merchant is sad and anxious; two of his friends sympathise with him and Salario declares:

> Your mind is tossing on the ocean,
> There, where your argosies with portly sail
> . . . Do overpeer the petty traffickers,
> That curtsy to them, do them reverence
> As they fly by them with their woven wings.

The other friend says that if he owned any ships:

> I should be still
> Plucking the grass, to know where sits the wind,
> Peering in maps for ports, and piers, and roads.

The only way that people in western Europe could hope to get spices more cheaply than through Venice was by importing them by ship direct from the east. The first European expedition to achieve this was commanded by a Portuguese Admiral, Vasco da Gama. His ships left Lisbon in 1497 amid great excitement. The Cape of Good Hope had been discovered and now he hoped to reach the west coast of India, the source of

Vasco da Gama opening up direct trade with India

almost all the pepper coming to Europe. He succeeded beyond all expectation, and at Goa on the west coast of India set up the headquarters of what quickly became the capital of a trade empire. His fame soon inspired another young man, Ferdinand Magellan, to join the crew of a ship that was leaving Lisbon for a voyage still further to the east—as far as Sumatra on the eastern side of the Indian Ocean, and perhaps even to the Spice Islands themselves. On this expedition Magellan, who fought in two minor wars and was twice wounded, distinguished himself by his courage and enterprise. He saw the wealth and prosperity of the East Indies and, as he had always spent much time 'peering in maps for ports', he returned to Portugal and asked the King to give him ships and men for an expedition round the south of South America and westwards across the Pacific so that he could enter the spice trade 'by the back door'. His plan was rejected as too dangerous, and so in 1519 he went to the King of Spain, who gave him what he wanted.

On the long voyage south of the Equator the weather became colder and colder and the seas stormier. Two of the ships asked to turn back, and mutinied when permission was refused. In the ensuing fight Magellan defeated the mutineers and executed their leaders. He then threaded his way through the dangerous straits that bear his name. Fierce winds rushing down from snow-capped mountains nearly drove them back. The water was too deep to anchor in and the force of the tide threatened to carry them on to the rocky shore. At last they were out in the Pacific, an ocean that for once lived up to its name. For weeks they sailed peacefully westwards, hoping to find land; their food had almost gone and many men had died before they reached the East Indies. There they became entangled in a tribal war, and Magellan was killed. Only one of his five ships got back to Spain, and, of the 243 men who had set out, only eighteen were still alive when she tied up at the quay in Seville, but they were the first men to circumnavigate the world and in the hold of their little ship was a cargo of cloves that sold for enough money to repay the whole cost of fitting out the expedition.

Magellan's men declared that the clove trees with their dark green shining foliage and fragrant golden-yellow flowers were the most beautiful trees in the world. The tiny flower buds are picked before they open and then dried, but the fragrance of the trees still remains locked up inside them. They are used to flavour apple dishes, hams and pickles, and their name is derived from the Latin word *clavus* which means a nail, since they are so hard and pointed that they resemble small nails.

The English did not break into the spice trade until nearly a hundred years after Magellan's voyage. The first man to show the way was Sir Francis Drake, who in 1577 followed Magellan's route into the Pacific. His exploits in the *Golden Hind* against the Spaniards on the coast of Peru are well known, but his achievements on the voyage home are equally astonishing. First he sailed up the west coast of America to latitude 43°N. Then he crossed the Pacific to the Moluccas, as the Spice Islands were called, where he was welcomed by the King of Ternate and seventy other islands and given, among other things, a large quantity of cloves. Unfortunately soon after he left, *Golden Hind* struck a reef. Instead of abandoning ship, Drake jettisoned three tuns of cloves and other cargo and, by lightening the ship a little, managed to refloat her. He then set sail for the Cape of Good Hope, guessing that the Spaniards would be on the look-out for him with a large force if he tried to return by way of South America. In November 1580, after a

Sir Francis Drake

three-year voyage, he sailed into Plymouth Sound with all his loot, having circumnavigated the world and incidentally become the first Englishman to bring back spices direct from the east.

In the year of Drake's return the King of Portugal died without any heir and the King of Spain, Philip II, took over the country, but this did not at first make much difference to the Portuguese colonies. Spices were still reaching Europe by two routes, through the ports of Syria and Egypt, where the Venetians were dominant, and by sea from the Moluccas and Goa, and so in 1583 a London merchant, Ralph Fitch, and three companions decided to travel to the east and see for themselves how the trade was conducted and what the prices were in the various markets on the way.

They sailed as passengers on the *Tiger*, bound for Syria. Their first objective was the town of Aleppo, where the camel caravans came in from the east like ships of the desert. From

Camel caravan from the east

there they travelled by way of the river Tigris to the head of the Persian Gulf and on to Ormuz at its mouth, an island on which the Portuguese had built a castle in order to control the traders of various nationalities, including Venetians, who dealt there in spices, silks, pearls and jewels. When the Englishmen, one of whom was a jeweller, arrived and set up a shop, the Venetians became extremely jealous. They were seized and brought before the governor of the castle on a charge of spying. To save them from the Venetians, the governor, who had once received a handsome present from an Englishman, sent them under guard to be tried by the Portuguese Viceroy in Goa.

The Viceroy kept them in close confinement and sent a Jesuit priest from Bruges, who spoke English well, to interrogate them. Their story that they were not Protestants, but, like the Portuguese, Catholics, had not been believed, but the Jesuit was convinced that they were speaking the truth and, finding that one of them was a painter, he obtained his release so that he might decorate the interior of a new church. Later an English Jesuit arranged for the others to be released on condition that they continued to live in the town and wait for trial. This gave them a wonderful opportunity to watch the embassies from native kings come and go. Those from the East Indies showed every sign of dignity and great wealth.

Fitch noticed and remembered everything. He knew that cooks at home grated nutmegs to flavour pies and custards; now he learned that a nutmeg was the hard kernel of a fruit

36

that grew on the island of Banda; its fleshy outer covering, dried and ground, another spice called mace. The countless possibilities for trade made him impatient. He complained of the delay in bringing his party to trial. The Viceroy, hearing of this, angrily let it be known that they were in danger of the strappado. Fitch and two others decided to escape. They sold all they had to obtain jewels and, pretending that they were going out into the country for the day, took a guide with them and slipped across the border and out of Portuguese territory. The painter stayed in Goa, married and settled down. Of the remaining two the jeweller obtained a well paid post at the court of an Indian prince and the other died. Ralph Fitch journeyed on alone across India to Bengal, took ship for Burma and, after staying there for a time, went to Malacca, a Portuguese trading station in Malaya. On his journey home he again stayed in Burma, and even re-visited Goa and Ormuz without being recognised. He then returned by way of Aleppo and reached London after an absence of eight years.

The tale of his adventures aroused immense interest. Since Drake's return from the Moluccas the Spanish Armada had been defeated, and men's thoughts were turning once more to ocean trade. A long book was being published about English sailors, travellers and explorers and to this Fitch contributed a short account of the countries he had seen and their inhabitants. Shakespeare probably read this, and later, in writing the third scene in *Macbeth*, put these words into the mouth of one of the witches:

> *Her husband's to Aleppo gone, master o'the Tiger;*
> *But in a sieve I'll thither sail . . .*
> *Though his bark cannot be lost,*
> *Yet shall it be tempest-tost.*

4
Tcha, Cophee and Xocolatl

The first advertisement for tea printed in England appeared in London in 1658 and read:

> That Excellent, and by all Physitians approved China Drink called by the Chineans Tcha, by other nations Tay, alias Tee, sold at the Sultaness-head, a cophee house in Sweetings Rents by the Royal Exchange in London.

The name of the proprietor was Thomas Garway, and his customers either sat and drank their tea in his shop or sent a servant with a jug to be filled at his tea urn and re-heated in their offices. This is not the way to get a good cup of tea, and tea did not become popular so quickly as coffee, which began to be sold in London about the same time. Tea, being made from the dried leaves of a plant which botanists call *camellia sinensis*, needs to be made with skill. There are a number of different China teas each with its own peculiar flavour, some coming from 'black' and some from 'green' leaf.

The Portuguese, who were the first Europeans to reach China by sea, noticed that people of all ranks much enjoyed tea-drinking. Rich people had over twenty different utensils and pieces of china for making and serving it. According to

Above: (left) tea plant, (centre) coffee plant, (right) cacao beans

some, the first Emperor to drink tea had done so in 2737 BC. Yet it was not a pleasure that the Chinese were ready to share with any nation, since they considered all races but their own uncivilised and at first refused to do any trade with them.

The Portuguese, however, persuaded the mandarins in Canton to allow them to set up a trading station at Macao. The ordinary Chinese found that the foreigners were prepared to pay in silver coin for everything they took away, and that the mandarins, as the Portuguese called the Chinese officials, would, for a consideration, forget about the imperial decrees ordering the barbarians to depart. Macao was an isolated spot on the coast some distance from Canton and the precious tea gardens were far away in the interior where no stranger need be allowed to go. Ships could only get to Canton, a city of a million inhabitants built on the north bank of the Pearl river, by way of a rocky gorge six miles long and little more than a mile wide, a passage made difficult to navigate by tidal currents and commanded by shore batteries.

In 1637 these happy arrangements were disturbed by an Englishman, Captain Weddell, who arrived at Macao with three ships, eager to trade. He found himself unwelcome both

One way in which a wealthy Portuguese travelled when abroad

to the Portuguese and Chinese. Violent quarrels broke out. The Chinese forts fired at the English and the English fired back. The Chinese gunpowder was so weak that some of the shot just rolled out of the cannon's mouth, but Weddell's guns did considerable destruction, for which he had to apologise in order to obtain the release of three merchants who had gone ashore from his ships. They departed with only a small quantity of goods which they could have bought much more cheaply in the East Indies, but one of his party afterwards wrote that, while ashore, he had been given 'a certain drink called Chaa, which is only water with a kind of herb boiled in it. It must be drunk warm and is accounted wholesome.'

At the same time that the first tea reached England, Oliver Cromwell, who had ruled for five years as Lord Protector, died. After an interval of two years Charles II was made king and, fortunately for the tea merchants of London, he married a Portuguese princess, Catherine of Braganza, whose favourite drink was tea. This set the fashion, and though tea was very expensive the demand for it never stopped growing. In 1664 the price for 2 lb 2 oz was ninety-five shillings at a time when a shilling would buy a good dinner. The price included, with the cost of shipping, a tax, which could only be avoided by smuggling. Trade in contraband tea eventually became almost an industry, especially as the law did not allow anyone who was not a member of the East India Company to import tea.

In 1685 a new Emperor in China realised that it would be extremely profitable to relax some of the restrictions on trade with foreigners, and in 1689 the East India Company imported tea direct from Amoy, where it was called tea in the local dialect, pronounced tay, not tcha as in Cantonese. The system of buying was still extremely complicated and difficult for a

A 17th century painting of an English family at tea

foreigner to understand, especially as none of them were permitted to employ a teacher of Chinese. To control the business done with foreigners in Canton the Emperor appointed an official who in return gave him a large present on his birthday and other occasions, amounting to tens of thousands of pounds. In other words this official bought his position, and then appointed up to eight merchants, called the Hong, who gave him large presents in return for the special privilege of being the only ones allowed to trade with merchants from abroad. They in turn exacted various payments from all the ships entering and leaving port according to their size and tonnage.

Though the Hong were known to be rich, nobody could be quite sure that they were legally entitled to all the payments they demanded because all business was transacted in pidgin English, a strange language in which all sorts of Indian, Chinese and Portuguese words were mixed with English and pronounced in English fashion. In pidgin the Emperor's representative was called the Grand Hoppo and no ship could leave port before all taxes, dues and gratuities had been paid and the Grand Hoppo had issued his permission to sail, a document known as the Grand Chop. Many a captain, watching the weather and anxious to catch the monsoon wind for his voyage home, felt like paying almost anything to get the Chop.

To be given command of an East Indiaman was the ambition of most captains in the merchant marine. Not only did the Company pay them well but it allowed them to buy and sell enough Chinese goods on their own account to become rich men. The crew were allowed five per cent of the ship's capacity in which to stow what they bought, most of which was taken by the captain. As the ships were some of the biggest afloat, 500 to 600 tons, this was a valuable privilege. The captain of the *St George*, for example, when he was loading at Canton in 1748, put on board as his own purchases 55 chests and 150 rolls of China-ware and 117 boxes and tubs of tea; the chief mate had five tubs of tea, and the third mate one. After four or five voyages like this, each of which took about eighteen months, most captains were rich men.

From the earliest days the British Government had charged an import duty on tea. The amount varied from time to time, and in 1772 the East India Company, being nearly bankrupt, asked the Government to allow them to re-export tea from their London warehouse to the North American colonies duty free. The Company had been spending too much on building new ships and had a huge surplus of unsold tea on their hands. The Government consented; it had just had a long dispute with the colonials over taxation, and British goods of all kinds were being boycotted. Possibly cheap tea would be welcome, but the Government had in fact given the East India Company a monopoly and enabled them to sell tea more cheaply than any colonial merchant.

Anti-British propaganda in America made the most of this mistake. Excited mobs collected in Boston, one of the biggest ports, and when three English ships docked with tea on board, gangs dressed up as Red Indians forced their way into the holds, broke open the tea chests and tipped all the tea into the harbour. Some called this the Boston Tea Party; others realised that such riotous behaviour could not be allowed to go on, but it was too late. British troops, sent out to restore order, found that the mobs had got firearms. Shots were exchanged, and soon a civil war had developed. The French and Spanish joined in against the British. Britain lost all her American colonies; the United States of America was founded. Sometimes a quarrel is called 'a storm in a teacup'; this one was a tempest that split the English-speaking world apart.

Ocean trade between the United States, Britain and China soon recovered from the war and faster sailing ships were built for it. Those of the 1700s were very broad in comparison with their length. Those of the 1800s were longer and carried more and bigger sails. The new ships, which looked more like big racing yachts than trading vessels, were called clippers. In 1850

A drawing of the Boston Tea Party, 1773

the first of them entered London docks. This was the American clipper *Oriental* and she had made the voyage from the Canton river via the Cape of Good Hope, 9,000 miles, in only ninety-seven days. She had on board 1,118 tons of tea, which sold at better prices in the London auctions than any other tea. In the same year the first British tea clipper, the *Stornoway*, was launched in Aberdeen. She had been ordered by the foremost British firm trading in the Far East, Jardine, Matheson and Co.

Soon an annual tea race was held, six or seven clippers bound for London leaving Canton river on the same tide. News of their departure reached England overland through India and Egypt, but usually nothing more was heard of them till the leaders were sighted in the English Channel some three months later. By then the excitement along the south coast and in London was intense. The names and achievements of the ships and their captains were as well known as those of horses and jockeys in the Derby and innumerable bets were placed on their chances. Everybody watched the wind and studied the tide tables, for speed over the last part of the voyage through the Channel and into the Thames depended on both.

Rivalry between captains reached its peak in the race of 1866. The first two ships sighted off Cornwall were *Taeping* and *Ariel*. They raced up the Channel together, picked up steam tugs off Dungeness, and tied up in London within twenty minutes of each other. *Taeping* docked first, but, to the fury of her captain and crew, was judged to have tied with *Ariel*. Rather than dispute this verdict, the owners of the two ships preferred to share the valuable bonus of ten shillings a ton awarded by the tea merchants for the first cargo landed.

The last of the tea races came only five years later. It was won by *Titania* with a run of ninety-seven days from Foochow, the

The great clipper race between 'Taeping' (on the left) and 'Ariel'

same time as the American *Oriental* on her voyage twenty-one years before. Sailing ships were beginning to give way to ocean-going steamships, although it was still a long time before a steamship could go faster than a clipper with the wind behind her.

Tea-drinking in Britain was not restricted even in the eighteenth century to the wealthy. In 1797 Sir Frederic Eden, author of *The State of the Poor*, wrote:

> *Any person who will give himself the trouble of stepping into the cottages of Middlesex and Surrey at meal-times will find that, in poor families, tea is not only the usual beverage in the morning and evening but is generally drunk in large quantities at dinner.*

Much of the China tea poor people bought had been smuggled into the country to avoid duty. They did not throw away the leaves after each brew, so the tea they drank was often weak, but where a man's total income was £40 a year it was quite common for him to spend as much as £2, or five per cent of it, on tea.

In 1833 the Government took the China tea monopoly away from the East India Company, but soon afterwards planters went up into the Assam hills between India and Burma, persuaded the tribesmen to cut down the forests, which grow luxuriantly in the warm, wet climate, to dig the soil and to plant tea bushes. The tribesmen did both the tree-felling and the digging with the same tool, a strange cross between a sword, an axe and a spade. The experiments were a great success and the tea could be marketed in Britain more cheaply than China tea. By 1872 British planters with British capital had cleared over 300,000 acres and were sending home over 14,000,000 lb of tea a year.

This skill in tea planting also benefited the British-held island of Ceylon, where the tropical heat and plentiful rain made the high hills very suitable for tea. The first crops were gathered in the 1870s and by 1900 Ceylon and Indian teas were overtaking China tea in popularity. Since then the fall of the Chinese Empire and endless political troubles have still further reduced the China tea trade. The phrase 'all the tea in China' once described riches so vast that nobody could count them.

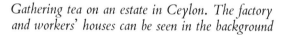

Gathering tea on an estate in Ceylon. The factory and workers' houses can be seen in the background

Today most tea comes from India and Ceylon, and more than half of all the tea grown in the world is drunk in Britain.

Coffee, which is made from the berries of a tropical shrub, was known as a stimulating food before it became a popular drink. The berries grow in small clusters close to the stem and resemble cherries, but instead of having one round white stone they have two half-round stones, or beans, each with a flat side that fits to the other. Warriors in Uganda, where coffee grows wild, used to extract the beans, roll them in fat and take them on campaigns. When they felt weary, they could, by chewing the beans, get the same stimulating effect as when the berries are roasted to a brown colour, ground to powder and brewed with boiling water. Twin beans taken from the same berry were regarded as symbols of blood brotherhood. If two warriors wished to become blood brothers, each would take one of a pair of beans, draw some of his own blood, dip the bean in it and exchange it with the other's bean, which he would then eat. After this they regarded themselves as eternally united.

Coffee-drinking became popular in Arabia in the 1400s. Moslem priests at first denounced the habit, saying that the new beverage was alcoholic. The holy book of the Moslems, the Koran, did not mention coffee, but it forbade Moslems to touch any kind of alcoholic liquor. Perhaps in brewing coffee some of the dried flesh of the coffee berry, fermented by the hot sun, had been added to the ground beans, and so made the drink slightly alcoholic. In any case the priests could not stop such a popular pastime as coffee-drinking. Arabian farmers took their coffee to Mocha at the southern end of the Red Sea for export and soon pilgrims passing through on their way to Mecca had spread the coffee habit to Cairo, Damascus, Aleppo

and Istanbul, the capital of the Turkish Empire, which then included a large part of eastern Europe. Soon Vienna and Paris had coffee houses.

In 1652 a London merchant, Daniel Edwards, who traded with Turkey, served his friends with coffee in his own house. It was brewed for him by a boy called Pasca Rosee, who had been born in Dubrovnik but had learned all about coffee in the Turkish port of Izmir. Edwards's friends liked the new drink so much that they kept asking for more and could scarcely be persuaded to go home, so he bought Pasca a house in St Michael's Alley, Cornhill, where he could serve coffee to all comers. Three hundred years later the Lord Mayor of London unveiled a plaque to mark the place where Pasca's coffee house had stood.

By the reign of Charles II Pasca's was one of several thousand coffee houses and the king was very angry when he heard that the customers, as they sipped their coffee and discussed the latest news, gossip and scandal, also criticised him and his friends. An order was issued that the houses should be closed but this was so unpopular that it was cancelled. One of them, called Lloyd's, was in Tower Street near the waterfront and attracted seagoing folk and also experts in marine insurance, called underwriters. Lloyd died in 1713 but his coffee house business went on and in 1734 *Lloyd's List and Shipping Gazette* first appeared. This is really London's oldest newspaper, as it has been published every weekday since. The earliest editions contained details of the movements of ships all over the world, news of wrecks, notes on any wars or political changes that might make insurance more expensive and many other matters. *Lloyd's List* still contains exact measurements of ships and details of their carrying capacity, age and seaworthiness. Since the beginning of air travel Lloyd's have also insured airliners and their cargoes. 'A1 at Lloyd's' has become an expression used all over the world to describe anything or anybody who is in first-class condition. It was first used in a coffee house.

Just as tea planting spread from China to other countries so coffee was taken from Arabia eastwards to India, Ceylon and the East Indies, south to Kenya, and west to the West Indies and Brazil. The coffee plant is very susceptible to changes in temperature and the quality and taste of the bean vary according to the climate and soil. White settlers in Kenya in the 1930s won prizes against world competition for the coffee they grew in the district round Mount Kilimanjaro, a huge extinct volcano which lies near the Equator, and yet is so high that the top of its cone is always covered with snow and ice. Farmers in Brazil found coffee an easy crop to grow and now produce so much that in a good year they could supply enough to meet the demands of the whole world, but many of them do not grow good quality coffee and are very poor; they starve in the midst of plenty.

The custom of drinking chocolate arrived in London from Mexico by way of Spain and France soon after coffee and tea. In 1657 a Frenchman, whose shop was in Bishopsgate, sold solid chocolate at ten to fifteen shillings a pound, and this was grated and dissolved in boiling water with sugar added. The diarist Samuel Pepys said after his first taste of 'jocolatte' that it was 'very good'. About 1700 the English began serving it with milk or cream and it gradually became a favourite drink in rich men's clubs. It truly deserved to be poured out from golden jugs into golden goblets, as it had once been at the court of the last Aztec Emperor of Mexico, Montezuma. He and his courtiers called it *xocolatl* and liked it so much that it was served both at and between meals, but with spices added, not sugar. For them it was a pleasantly bitter drink, and the Spaniards, who invaded their country in 1519 and destroyed Montezuma's empire, soon found out how to make it.

First the big fruit pods of the cacao tree were cut off the trunk and branches where they formed from small pink flowers

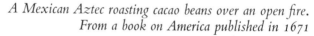

A Mexican Aztec roasting cacao beans over an open fire.
From a book on America published in 1671

sprouting directly from the bark. The pods were like cucumbers to look at and when split open lengthwise the seeds, or nibs, numbering twenty to fifty, lay in a gummy liquid that turned white on exposure to the sun and after two or three days fermented. This 'cooked' the nibs, and they were then pounded and stewed. The heat extracted an oil, which on cooling became a white fat called cocoa butter, and the nibs were then reboiled to brew xocolatl.

The Spaniards kept the secret of making chocolate to themselves when they sent the nibs home, and so it did not become known as a drink outside Spain for a long time. When the Dutch and the English captured Spanish ships and found sacks of chocolate on board, they threw them into the sea. The Spaniards also learnt how to flavour their chocolate with vanilla, that is, the thin dark seed pods of a climbing orchid cultivated by the Mexicans (*vainilla* in Spanish means 'little pod').

Vanilla eventually became the best-loved flavouring in the whole world, not only for chocolate but for all kinds of good things. For a long time all efforts to grow vanilla outside Mexico failed for a reason that could not be discovered. At last it was found that a tiny insect lived on the orchid and fertilised its flowers. In a foreign country without the insect the flowers were always barren until a French gardener tried fertilising the flowers by hand with a small brush. Vanilla transported to the French colony of Réunion, sometimes called Bourbon, an island in the Indian Ocean over 400 miles east of Madagascar, seeded well, and Bourbon vanilla is still the best in the world.

The first big manufacturers of chocolate in England were Fry's of Bristol. In 1730 they were selling plain chocolate at five shillings a pound and vanilla-flavoured at six shillings. The firm was then using water power, but in 1795 they bought the first steam engine to be employed in a chocolate mill.

In 1800 a member of the Fry family married Elizabeth Gurney of Norwich, who was twenty at the time and a Quakeress, though not a strict one, and they went to live in London. As a girl she had been fond of going to dances and wearing gay clothes—scarlet boots for riding and the big hats then fashionable. Later she adopted the plain grey dress and bonnet usually worn by Quakers. A friend took her to see the women prisoners in Newgate gaol, which was near her home. They were kept in horrible squalor in one big room, noisily gambling and quarrelling all day and sleeping on the bare stone floor. No one believed it possible to reform such women, but Elizabeth Fry first collected warm clothes and blankets for them and, having won their confidence, began to teach them to read, write and sew. Her Quaker friends helped her greatly in this work and her advice was sought by the Government and by foreign countries. It is nowhere recorded whether she gave her prisoners chocolate, but it would have been in keeping with her homely, practical ways to have done so. No sensible person, after seeing what she had achieved, could think it right to allow criminals to be treated badly in prison, however necessary it was to deprive them of their freedom.

The stand of J. S. Fry & Sons at the Manchester Exhibition of 1887

5
Potatoes

When the Spanish army under Francisco Pizarro invaded Peru and overthrew the empire of the Incas in 1532, they not only acquired gold and silver in vast quantities, but also discovered a new food crop which eventually proved more valuable to the world than all the precious metal mined in America, namely potatoes.

The Inca empire stretched for over 3,000 miles along the whole range of the Andes, their towns and fortresses clinging to precipitous mountains, with summits often hidden in clouds of sleet and snow. It included not only the territory of the modern republic of Peru but large parts of Ecuador, Bolivia and Chile and was inhabited by many different Indian tribes, most of them clever farmers as long as the Incas were there to organise them. Left to themselves, they lapsed into hopeless lethargy. They had never seen horses (those the Spaniards brought terrified them) and had no wheeled vehicles or ploughs, and llamas, used as pack animals to take goods to market, could not carry more than 100 lb each. Their only tools were copper-bladed digging sticks and hoes, yet with these they grew maize,

Above: Inca pottery vessel showing a labourer going to till the fields. Hand tools were used for the plough was unknown

avocados, papaya and pineapple in the warm tropical valleys and, up in the mountains, potatoes. Here frost on growing plants killed them, and if the temperature in a potato store fell below zero the whole became useless. The Indians therefore dehydrated their potatoes by stamping on them to release the moisture and then alternately drying and freezing them, producing a white powder called *chuño* which was easy to transport and could, by adding boiling water, be made into a nourishing dish; with butter, milk and spices instead of water it was delicious.

Chuño played a big part in the development of Peru. In 1545 a shepherd was herding on the slopes of Mount Potosi. The foot of this mountain is as high above sea level as the highest peak in Europe and, though it lies well within the tropics, the weather even in summer is always cool and windy. Naturally at night the shepherd lit a fire and in the morning he found patches of silver underneath the warm ashes. He told his master, Juan de Villarvel, who at once registered a claim with the Spanish government. When mining began it was found that the huge sugar-loaf mountain was so rich in silver ore that, no matter where the soil was moved, more ore was found. The news spread like a forest fire. Hundreds of fortune hunters began to arrive from other Spanish colonies and from Europe and a town sprang up at the base of the mountain. Every ounce of food for the newcomers had to be carried there from other parts of Peru, for no food plant would grow at such an altitude. Chuño became a staple food for the Potosinos. For those who grew rich on silver no luxury was considered too expensive to import.

Every stage in the development of Potosi was reported to the Emperor Charles V and his son Philip II, and their officials

*Workers in a silver mine in Mount Potosi, vividly portrayed
by an 18th century artist from earlier reports*

sent out from Spain elaborate instructions for its government
and the minting of the silver. Charles V gave it the title Villa
Imperial, '*El rico Potosi, el tresoro del mundo, el rey de las montanas,
y la envidia de los reyes*' (Rich Potosi, treasure of the world, the
king of mountains and the envy of kings). Fine law courts, a
royal mint and beautiful churches, all dating from the 16th
century, are still to be seen in the streets. Millions of pounds'
worth of silver were sent back to Spain, but the people of
Potosi spent much of their time in quarrelling and rioting, one
gang against another. The mountain itself was becoming like a
honeycomb as miners dug into it from every direction and
many lives were lost as the shafts became deeper or their sides
fell in.

The method of separating silver from its ore most favoured
in the 1600s was called the amalgam method. The ore was put

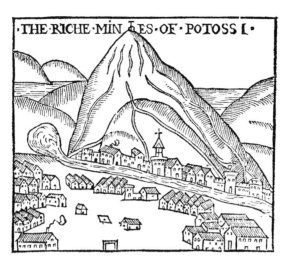

Woodcut from the title page of a 16th century history of Peru

with some water on to the stone floor of a circular pit with a central post on which rotated a beam and a mule, walking in a circle round the pit, ground the ore to a fine paste. It was then taken out and spread in low heaps all over a stone-paved courtyard or patio and sprinkled with mercury, salt and copper sulphate. Mules were then driven to and fro across the heaps for about a month, mixing them together. At the end of this process the silver and mercury had amalgamated. Mercury, being, unlike other metals, a liquid at ordinary temperatures and extremely heavy, could easily be washed out of the waste with the silver clinging to it, and then separted from the silver by evaporation and condensation, since mercury boils at a temperature much lower than the melting point of silver.

Most of the mercury from this process could be used again and again but for such a large mine as Potosi, one of the richest ever discovered in the world, there was a great demand for additional supplies. Here again the Spaniards were most fortunate. In 1563 a mercury mine was discovered at Huancavelica, much nearer Lima than Potosi, and found to be one of the three most productive in the world. Between it and Potosi lay many miles of mountain road, but also Lake Poopo, where there were immense natural deposits of salt, and so the extraction of silver went on faster than ever until in the 18th century the mine was exhausted.

The usefulness of potatoes, however, had yet to be learned. How they reached the British Isles is a mystery. Several English seamen saw and tasted potatoes in South America, but there is no proof that they imported any. Sir Francis Drake reported that the natives of the island of Mocha off the coast of Chile (38°31′ south latitude), where he landed on 28 November 1577, 'came down to the water side with show of great courtesy, bringing us potatoes, roots and two very fat sheep'. Nearly ten years later Thomas Cavendish, who called at St Mary Island, near the Chilean port of Concepción, found 'cases of straw

Francis Drake (left), Thomas Cavendish (centre) and a contemporary explorer John Hawkins, a painting by an unknown artist

filled with potatoes, which were very good to eat, in store-houses for the Spanish against the time they should come for this tribute'.

It is not known whether Drake or Cavendish was able to bring any potatoes home. If they did, Sir Walter Raleigh may have 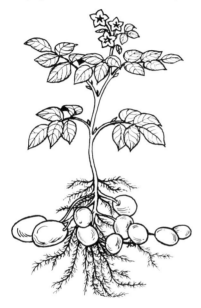 acquired some, for he was always looking out for new things from America. Possibly he acquired potatoes from Virginia, which had recently been explored under his direction. A learned book about plants called Gerard's *Herbal*, published in 1597 and dedicated to Raleigh, described the potato and said that it came from Virginia. At this time Raleigh, with his usual energy and inventiveness, was developing the estates that Queen Elizabeth had given him near Youghal in southern Ireland. He had settled 120 Englishmen, brought in Cornish miners to exploit minerals, drained bogs and perhaps planted potatoes. Certainly fifty years later more potatoes were grown in Ireland than anywhere else and the poor became accustomed to a diet of potatoes and milk; this kept them healthy but led to bad farming habits. They relied on one crop only, like peasants in Bengal, where if the monsoon fails to bring rain at the right time the rice crop withers away and the whole population starves. In 1845 a blight struck a large part of the Irish potato

Potato plant

crop. In London the Prime Minister, Sir Robert Peel, called for a scientific report on its causes and extent and made arrangements for Government purchases of maize in the USA to be shipped to Cork and distributed to those in need. No way of preventing the blight was discovered for many years, and nobody realised how serious the results of the blight in 1845 would be. Often potatoes that had appeared to be sound when harvested and stored became rotten during the winter, and too few sound ones were kept for seed.

A Government organisation, created with great speed, carried relief to the famine areas and kept over three million people alive, but it was not strong enough to prevent a disaster.

The summer of the next year, 1846, was very wet and the blight returned, spreading over the whole island in a few weeks. One month fields appeared healthy, the next they were a mass of rottenness. Starving farm-workers crowded together in towns and villages hoping that the Government would send help in time. Being weak with hunger and unable to wash, they fell victim to epidemics of typhus and cholera. Thousands died and hundreds of thousands crowded on to ships sailing to North America or Australia, where they took the worst-paid work in order to survive.

Emigrant to Australia,
mid 19th century

In the USA and Canada the authorities became alarmed at the risk of contagious diseases. Many Irish perished either on board ship or in the quarantine quarters where they were confined on arrival. In Montreal a great mound marks the grave of 6,000 such migrants. Few Irish were ever able to earn enough money to return home, but they retained a great love for Ireland and a hatred of the British, blaming them for not having averted the effects of the potato disease. In their adopted countries they were able to vote in elections, and the politicians whom they supported, especially in the United States, were frequently anti-British. The potato famine had undermined the British Empire, just as the wheat rust weakened the Roman Empire.

About thirty-five years later it was discovered that the blight had been caused by a fungus. Its spores, like the spores of wheat rust, were carried by the wind and multiplied very rapidly in warm, wet weather. Fortunately a Welsh farmer noticed that potato fields lying downwind from a chemical works remained free from blight, and it was supposed that the fumes of copper sulphate had killed the fungus spores. Later, sprays of copper sulphate and lime were used to protect crops, and many experiments were made to improve the various breeds of seed potatoes.

Not until the eighteenth century did potatoes become an important crop on the continent of Europe. In 1764 the King of Sweden issued an edict ordering his subjects to grow potatoes. About the same time the Prussians began to grow them in order to overcome the food shortages caused by the Seven Years' War. In most countries poor people were at first suspicious of potatoes and did not think them good to eat. In France Louis XVI, the king whom revolutionaries later guillotined, was very anxious that they should be widely grown. According to one story, he planted them in the gardens of his palace at Versailles. When the crop was nearly ready to be harvested, he gave secret orders to the palace guard to mount sentries all round the gardens, but to call them in at night. The peasants in the neighbourhood watched these precautions and came to the conclusion that the tubers must be very valuable, and so during the hours of darkness they crept in and stole them. The French name for potatoes, *pommes de terre*, shows how popular they became.

Louis XVI

6
Meals at Historic Moments

Some of the oldest history books in the world are to be found in the Bible. They contain the earliest accounts that the Israelites were able to preserve of the laws and customs which made them from ancient times a race apart, different from all their neighbours. Many of these laws concerned food and the way to prepare it, not only for everyday, but for special occasions, including the most sacred of all their festivals, Passover.

According to the second book of the Bible, *Exodus*, the first Passover was observed at the end of their long stay in Egypt—430 years after the wheat famine. By then they had fallen into the bitterest slavery, being driven by taskmasters armed with whips to carry out vast building projects. At last they found a leader, Moses, who decided to take them out of Egypt into the desert, and asked the Pharaoh's permission to do so. Again and again the Pharaoh refused, though Moses warned him that it was contrary to the will of God that he should keep them in captivity. The Egyptians consequently suffered a series of plagues. Before the last of these Moses ordered his people to be ready for a sudden departure, a march on which they were to take only what they needed to prepare food, nothing else. On a certain night each household was to kill a young lamb or goat and dip a sprig of marjoram in its blood. With this they were to mark the doorposts of their houses. Then they were to roast the flesh and eat it in haste with bitter herbs and unleavened bread.

On the appointed evening the first-born child in every Egyptian house died, including the Pharaoh's son, but there were no deaths in the houses marked with blood. Next day the Pharaoh ordered all the Israelites to leave immediately and the Egyptians did everything they could to speed their departure. Marching eastwards into the desert round Mount Sinai they had passed safely through the marshes at the northern end of the Red Sea when they heard that the Pharaoh was pursuing them with his whole army and all his chariots. Only a sudden flood, blown in from the sea by a gale of wind, and filling all the

A Jewish family from Arabia keeping Passover. The Passover candle, the wine and the round unleavened bread can be seen

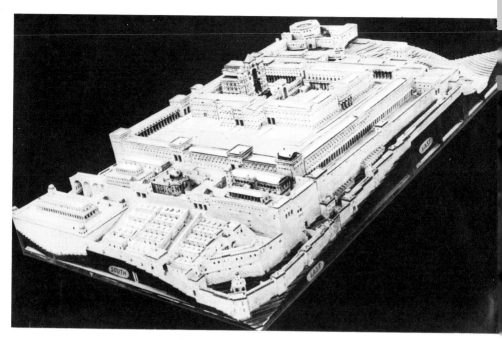

*A model showing how Solomon's Temple at Jerusalem,
and the buildings near to it, may have looked*

marshes with deep water, saved them. The Pharaoh and his
army were drowned and the Jews, to commemorate this
escape, keep Passover every year. It is a spring festival and
occurs about the same time as the Christians celebrate Easter.

After forty years in the Sinai desert, the Israelites conquered
the land now called Israel and made Jerusalem their capital.
Solomon, the greatest of their kings, raised a splendid temple
on Mount Zion, and there the people of Judah worshipped
for over three hundred years, until, in 586 BC, Jerusalem was
captured and the temple destroyed by Nebuchadnezzar. He
made the homeland of the Jews part of his empire, and forced
them to leave and march a thousand miles to his capital,
Babylon on the Euphrates, where they were allowed to form a
colony. The Jews compared this Babylonian captivity with the

sufferings of their ancestors in Egypt and one of their poets
wrote:

By the rivers of Babylon, there we sat down, yea, we wept,
when we remembered Zion.
We hanged our harps upon the willows in the midst thereof.
For there they that carried us away captive required of us a song;
and they that wasted us required of us mirth, saying, Sing us one
of the songs of Zion.
How shall we sing the Lord's song in a strange land?

(Psalm 137, 1–4)

When Nebuchadnezzar died, his vast empire did not long
survive. It was overthrown by Cyrus, King of the Persians,
who encouraged the Jews in Babylon to go back to Jerusalem.
Some, but not all, did so. Those who remained were for a
century happy and prosperous under Persian rule. Then one of
them, Nehemiah, became the royal cupbearer, a high office.
In the Bible there is his own account of a banquet when the
king and queen were present:

I took up the wine and gave it to the king. Now I had not
before been sad in his presence and King Artaxerxes said to me,
Why is thy countenance sad, seeing that thou art not sick? This
is nothing but sorrow of the heart?

(Nehemiah 2, 1–2)

That one piercing question in the middle of a feast changed
the whole course of Jewish history. Nehemiah told the king
that he was sad because he had heard from friends in Jerusalem
that the Jews there were most unhappy, and needed help. The
king generously gave him leave to go to Jerusalem, taking over
a thousand Jews with him and a letter to the governor of that
region instructing him to allow Nehemiah freedom to act as he
thought best. The new settlers, after enduring much hardship

65

and danger, established themselves firmly in Jerusalem, built a second temple and strictly observed the laws handed down since the days of Moses. The city of Zion, as it was sometimes called, became a place of pilgrimage for Jews from many different parts of the world and continued to be so during the time of Christ's life on earth.

It is the test of a good leader whether he can speak and act with cheerful optimism when his followers are oppressed with doubt and fear. In this respect William the Conqueror proved worthy of his name during his campaign against England in 1066. All through the summer the Normans were building ships to transport their army and its horses across the Channel, but, when they were all ready, the wind blew steadily from the north and prevented them from leaving. They were encamped near the mouth of the river Somme and the ships were drawn up on the beach. What happened next is told by a Norman chronicler who knew Duke William well. On the afternoon of 27 September the wind suddenly changed. It was late in the

Scenes from the Bayeux Tapestry, medieval embroidery portraying the Norman invasion of England, and made only 20 years after the conquest. Food is prepared for William and his men. Meat is cooked over a fire; bread . . .

year and sailors knew that storms were likely to blow up
without warning, so the Duke ordered his men to embark
immediately. Evening came before all were on board, but the
Duke forbade them to set sail for England until he had gone to
the head of the fleet and hoisted a lantern at the top of his mast
to guide them. In the night his ship sailed faster than the rest;
at first light he sent one of his oarsmen up the mast to look for
the fleet. The man reported that there was nothing to be seen
but sea and sky. The danger was great; all on board knew that
they were near the English coast and that English warships
might come upon them; they also realised that, if part of the
fleet had changed course, they might make scattered landings
and be defeated piecemeal. The Duke alone remained calm and
ordered the anchor to be lowered. He then called for a large
meal and a bumper of spiced wine, which he enjoyed at leisure,
joking with his companions 'as if he were', the chronicler says,
'in a room of his house at home'. When he had finished the
oarsman climbed to the masthead again and reported four

. . . or cakes are served on a trencher; spits of meat are passed
to servants at a side table, one of whom blows a horn
to show that the food is ready. William and his
companions are at the high table and the meal begins

ships. A little later he cried out that the numberless masts clustered together looked like trees in a forest. With the wind still in their favour they all reached the beach at Pevensey in Sussex together, and, landing unopposed, camped within the high walls of the old Roman fort. During the next fortnight they moved to Hastings and scoured all the nearby villages for food. Very early on 14 October, after a six-mile march, they attacked King Harold's men, many of them weary after their long journey from York, and at the end of the day gained the whole kingdom by one complete victory.

Since 1066 enemy forces have landed from time to time on the coast of Britain but none have been victorious. One of the moments of greatest danger was in 1805 when the Emperor Napoleon assembled a splendid army in the downs near Boulogne and a fleet of flat-bottomed boats to carry them across the Channel for the conquest of Britain. To protect his army during the crossing he ordered the French navy to combine with that of the Spaniards, who were his allies, and enter the Channel in such force that the British could not attack. The French admirals were never able to carry out these orders. In October they were still far to the south, cooped up in Cadiz harbour with the English fleet under its second-in-command, Admiral Collingwood, hovering just over the horizon waiting for them to come out and give battle. It was already too late in the year for the French to attempt invasion.

On 28 September the British commander-in-chief, Admiral Lord Nelson on board *Victory*, joined the fleet. He ordered that he should not be given any special salute in case the enemy should hear of his arrival. The next day, being his forty-seventh birthday, he invited all his captains to dinner on board *Victory*. It was his custom to entertain them in this way—he called them

HMS 'Victory', as she can be seen today in Portsmouth harbour

in Shakespeare's words his 'band of brothers'. After dinner the table was cleared, leaving only the wine glasses and decanters, their heavy crystal bases keeping them firm as *Victory* rocked in the swell. Nelson said that he had something of the greatest importance to tell them. First, the Spaniards were incapable of getting sufficient supplies for the men of the combined fleet overland, the roads being too bad. Cadiz must therefore be blockaded to prevent the entry of food ships; then the enemy would be forced to sail and face battle. Secondly, he proposed to ignore the *Fighting Instructions* of the Royal Navy, a book regarded by officers of every rank as demanding the same obedience as the Ten Commandments. Before the coming fight their sailing order was to be two columns or divisions with *Victory* in the van of one and Collingwood's *Royal Sovereign* heading the other, and, contrary to *Fighting Instructions*, this formation was also to be their battle order. The two columns were to force their way through the centre of the enemy's line and cut it in two before their leading ships could be brought round into the fight. His aim was the total destruction of the enemy's fleet; he would not be content with anything less. The captains listened with enthusiasm, and Nelson wrote home: 'Some shed tears, all approved. It was new—it was singular—it was simple.'

On 19 October the enemy left Cadiz; on the 21st battle was joined off Cape Trafalgar, twelve Spanish and twenty-one French ships against Nelson's twenty-seven. By 4.30 in the afternoon, when firing ceased, eighteen enemy ships had surrendered and the rest were in full retreat. The plan agreed at Nelson's birthday dinner had brought complete victory, but the great Admiral, mortally wounded, died soon after hearing the news.

Admiral Collingwood's Trafalgar dispatch did not reach London until early in November. The coaches that carried the newspapers out from London were decked with laurels for victory and black for death. Nelson had been so popular that his loss almost overshadowed the rejoicings and the thankfulness that for the rest of the war Britain would be safe from invasion. On 9 November the Prime Minister, William Pitt, set out in his coach to attend the banquet given in the Guildhall in London by the new Lord Mayor, then, as now, an annual event to which the leading men in the Government were invited. This year the crowds, having heard the news of Trafalgar only a few days before, cheered Pitt through the streets and when he reached Cheapside they unharnessed the horses from his coach and pulled it themselves the rest of the way. When the Lord Mayor proposed Pitt's health, he called him the saviour of Europe. In reply Pitt said:

I return you thanks for the honour which you have paid me, but Europe is not to be saved by any single man. England has saved herself by her exertions and will, I trust, save Europe by her example.

The Duke of Wellington, remembering this occasion more than thirty years later, told a friend:

It was one of the best and neatest speeches I have ever heard in my life. He was not up for more than two minutes. Nothing could have been more perfect.

The Battle of Trafalgar, an 18th century painting. The French fleet in the foreground is retreating from the British lines, which are sailing into action from the right. The 'Victory', leading the nearer line, has broken the enemy formation

Index

Acknowledgements

The photograph on page 20 of the Great Hall of Hampton Court is reproduced by gracious permission of Her Majesty the Queen.

We are most grateful to the following bodies and individuals for permission to reproduce the illustrations.

British Museum, pages 9 (top), 23, 39; Ceylon Tea Centre, 43, 46; Chatto & Windus Ltd and Will Nickless, 26, 31; Colchester and Essex Museum, 12; Controller of HM Stationery Office (Crown copyright), 11; J. S. Fry & Sons, 50, 52; Lloyd's of London and Bertram Chapman, 48; Macdonald & Co Ltd, 59; Macmillan & Co Ltd, 55; Mary Evans Picture Library, 18; Parker Gallery, 45; Peruvian Embassy, 56; Phaidon Press Ltd, 66, 67; Paul Popper Ltd, 35, 63; Portsmouth City Corporation, 69; Musée de l'Homme, 53; National Film Board of Canada, 6, 7, 28, 29; National Maritime Museum, 57, 71; Radio Times Hulton Picture Library, 24, 27, 33, 61, 64; Tate Gallery, 41; Victoria and Albert Museum (Crown copyright), 22; Roy J. Westlake, 15.